24 HOUR HISTORY

D-DAY

6 JUNE 1944

Agnieszka Biskup

Raintree is an imprint of Capstone Global Library
Limited, a company incorporated in England and Wales
having its registered office at 7 Pilgrim Street, London,
EC4V 6LB – Registered company number: 6695582

www.raintreepublishers.co.uk
myorders@raintreepublishers.co.uk

Text © Capstone Global Library Limited 2014
First published in hardback in 2014
The moral rights of the proprietor have been asserted.

Edited by Adam Miller, Abby Colich, and
    John-Paul Wilkins
Designed by Steve Mead
Original illustrations © Advocate Art 2014
Illustrated by Warren Pleece
Production by Victoria Fitzgerald
Originated by Capstone Global Library Ltd
Printed and bound in China

ISBN 978 1 406 27365 6
18 17 16 15 14
10 9 8 7 6 5 4 3 2 1

A full catalogue record for this book is available from
the British Library.

Acknowledgements
We would like to thank Gerard DeGroot for his
invaluable help in the preparation of this book.

CONTENTS

Early 1944. Western Europe lies under the control of Nazi Germany.

Adolf Hitler is the Führer, or dictator, of Germany.

The Soviet Union fights Germany in the East, and the United States and Great Britain are across the English Channel preparing to invade occupied France.

The code name of their invasion plan is "Operation Overlord".

THE AXIS, ALLIES, AND WORLD WAR II

The war began on 1 September 1939, when Germany, led by Adolf Hitler and his Nazi Party, invaded Poland. France and Great Britain responded by declaring war on Germany, and two opposing alliances were formed: the Axis and the Allies. The Axis powers eventually included Germany, Italy, and Japan. The Allied powers included Great Britain, France, the United States, and (later) the Soviet Union. By the time the war was over, more than 50 million lives had been lost. It remains the deadliest conflict of all time.

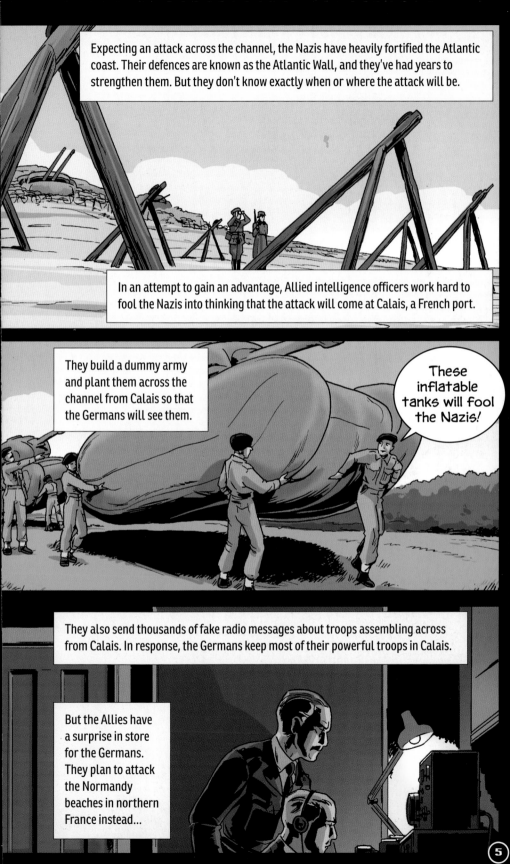

Expecting an attack across the channel, the Nazis have heavily fortified the Atlantic coast. Their defences are known as the Atlantic Wall, and they've had years to strengthen them. But they don't know exactly when or where the attack will be.

In an attempt to gain an advantage, Allied intelligence officers work hard to fool the Nazis into thinking that the attack will come at Calais, a French port.

They build a dummy army and plant them across the channel from Calais so that the Germans will see them.

These inflatable tanks will fool the Nazis!

They also send thousands of fake radio messages about troops assembling across from Calais. In response, the Germans keep most of their powerful troops in Calais.

But the Allies have a surprise in store for the Germans. They plan to attack the Normandy beaches in northern France instead...

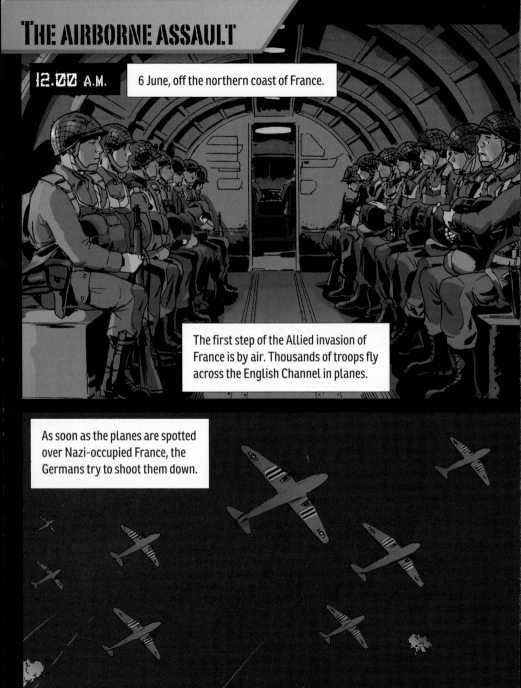

THE AIRBORNE ASSAULT

12.00 A.M. 6 June, off the northern coast of France.

The first step of the Allied invasion of France is by air. Thousands of troops fly across the English Channel in planes.

As soon as the planes are spotted over Nazi-occupied France, the Germans try to shoot them down.

12.15 A.M. Somewhere in Normandy, France...

Paratroopers that survive enemy fire have numerous dangerous missions to accomplish. Their main job is to gain control of areas so that troops can move inland safely when they arrive.

They do this by securing towns and crossroads, protecting bridges, and by attacking and killing enemies any chance they get.

Due to heavy German fire, some planes go off course or drop their men too early. Many men are separated from their units.

Some drown in fields flooded by the Germans to halt the progress of paratroopers.

Some soldiers lose all their gear during the jump. They are miles away from their comrades, lost in the French countryside, and deep in enemy territory.

Some are captured by German soldiers.

The Allies also use huge gliders to bring troops and equipment in across the channel. The gliders are quiet and carry more supplies than regular aircraft.

They are towed by other planes and then released.

12.30 A.M.

British troops from one of the first gliders to land capture two critical bridges over the Caen Canal and the Orne River.

Later that morning, larger gliders arrive with more supplies, including jeeps, tanks, and even bulldozers.

But the Germans are prepared for gliders, too. They set up obstacles in open fields to prevent landings, or damage gliders that do land.

2.30 A.M.

As the airborne assault continues, one unfortunate company from the 82nd Airborne Division lands in the German-occupied town of Ste. Mère-Église.

What's that in the sky?

Expecting the German soldiers to be asleep, the paratroopers are horrified to find they've been awakened by a burning building in the town square. The fire lights up the night sky.

The Germans spot the paratroopers floating down and they open fire.

Quickly! Kill them before they land!

Private John Steele's parachute catches on a church steeple. He hangs helplessly for two hours before being captured by the Germans.

Ste. Mère-Église would later be captured by US troops.

3.00 A.M.

German officers are unsure whether the airborne assault is an actual invasion or a diversion.

Is this the invasion? I thought it was to be at Calais!

The landings are so random. I can't tell what they're planning. Should we call the Führer to release troops from Caen?

But what if it's a false alarm? Dare we wake him?

To add to the confusion, the Allies had also dropped thousands of dummies by parachute all over Normandy to draw enemy fire.

Vive la Résistance!

The civilians who worked against the Nazi occupation of France were called the French Résistance. They were small groups of armed men and women and sometimes even children who did all they could to fight their military occupiers. Members of the Résistance published underground newspapers, gathered information for the Allies, helped rescue soldiers caught behind enemy lines, and committed sabotage.

The French Résistance is alerted to the coming invasion in a coded radio message from the British.

Cut the telephone and cable lines! The Nazis won't be able to communicate!

If one unit has any information, it won't be able to tell anybody else!

They also hamper the movement of Nazi troops by blowing up railway tracks.

This will stop the Nazis from bringing in more troops and supplies!

ROMMEL'S GONE

It did not help the Germans that Field Marshal Rommel, the officer in charge of repulsing an invasion, was absent. Due to bad weather, he assumed there wouldn't be an attack and went to visit his wife in Germany.

Frerking has just seen the largest fleet ever to be assembled. The Allied invasion fleet has over 5,000 ships, including minesweepers, converted liners, merchant ships, battleships, destroyers, and transport ships.

Many soldiers had been on transport ships for days in bad weather, waiting for the invasion order.

BLEUGH!

I've never felt so seasick in my life. These waters are too rough for me!

5.50 A.M. Every ship capable of firing begins firing at the German defences. The world seems like it is exploding from the bombardment.

KERBLAM!

KABOOM!

Eventually, the soldiers board a Higgins boat, or Landing Craft, Vehicle and Personnel (LCVP). The Higgins boat would get them ashore.

D-DAY
D-Day is a military term that stands for the day of any major attack. The Allied invasion of Nazi-occupied Normandy on 6 June 1944 is the most famous D-Day of them all.

The soldiers have been assured that the aerial bombings and naval bombardment will take out the big guns that would attack them. Expecting light resistance, they prepare to storm the beaches.

The Allies had a detailed plan for the land invasion of Normandy. More than 156,000 American, British, and Canadian troops were ferried across the channel to attack five different portions of the Normandy beaches. American forces would land on the two westernmost beaches in Normandy, code-named Omaha and Utah. The British and Canadians would land on the three beaches to the east, code-named Gold, Sword, and Juno.

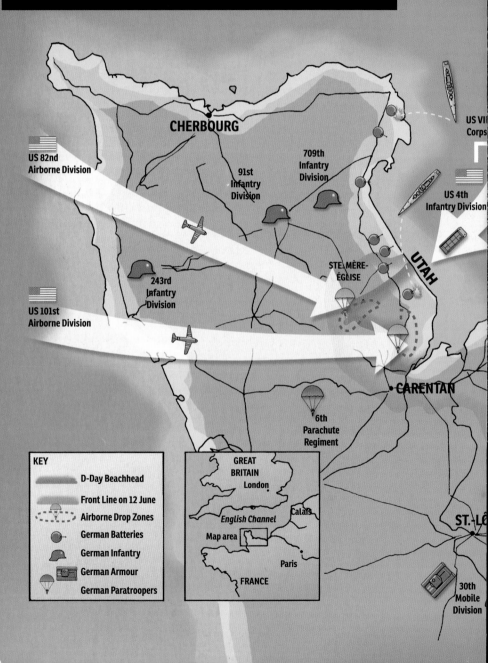

CHERBOURG

US 82nd
Airborne Division

US VII
Corps

709th
Infantry
Division

91st
Infantry
Division

US 4th
Infantry Division

243rd
Infantry
Division

STE. MÈRE-
ÉGLISE

UTAH

US 101st
Airborne Division

CARENTAN

6th
Parachute
Regiment

ST.-LÔ

KEY
- D-Day Beachhead
- Front Line on 12 June
- Airborne Drop Zones
- German Batteries
- German Infantry
- German Armour
- German Paratroopers

GREAT
BRITAIN
London

English Channel

Calais

Map area

Paris

FRANCE

30th
Mobile
Division

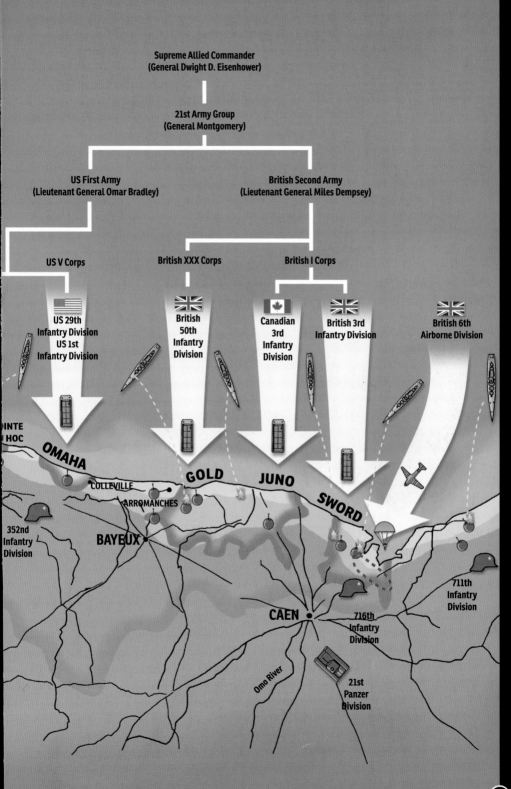

Supreme Allied Commander
(General Dwight D. Eisenhower)

21st Army Group
(General Montgomery)

US First Army
(Lieutenant General Omar Bradley)

British Second Army
(Lieutenant General Miles Dempsey)

US V Corps

British XXX Corps

British I Corps

US 29th
Infantry Division
US 1st
Infantry Division

British
50th
Infantry
Division

Canadian
3rd
Infantry
Division

British 3rd
Infantry Division

British 6th
Airborne Division

POINTE
DU HOC

OMAHA

COLLEVILLE

GOLD

JUNO

SWORD

ARROMANCHES

352nd
Infantry
Division

BAYEUX

711th
Infantry
Division

CAEN

716th
Infantry
Division

Omo River

21st
Panzer
Division

6.30 A.M.

The land assault of Omaha Beach begins.

Put this in your pack.

That's to bury you in, in case you need it.

What is it?

The steep cliffs surrounding the beach allow the Germans to fire down on the Allied troops. The failure of Allied bombers to hit the German bunkers above the beach leaves them hopelessly exposed. Many soldiers are hit before they even reach land.

Ten of the landing craft sink in the rough water.
Hundreds of men drown, weighed down by their gear.

Thirty-two specially equipped tanks meant to lead the assault are released too early. Twenty-nine of them sink straight away, along with their crews.

Soldiers who manage to dodge the bullets scramble for cover.

Some men are blown up when they step on mines. There is no break from the German gunfire that rains down from above.

The surviving men are scattered all over the beach. They are separated from their units, stumbling through the smoke of explosions and burning wreckage.

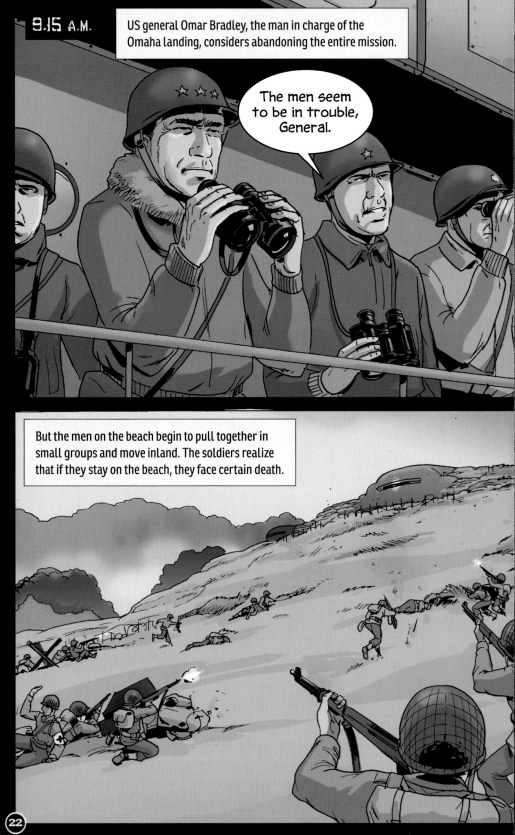

9.15 A.M. US general Omar Bradley, the man in charge of the Omaha landing, considers abandoning the entire mission.

The men seem to be in trouble, General.

But the men on the beach begin to pull together in small groups and move inland. The soldiers realize that if they stay on the beach, they face certain death.

Colonel Charles D. W. Canham, who commands the 116th Infantry Regiment, waves groups of men forward, as he walks upright along the beach in the face of enemy fire.

I'm more scared of Canham than the Germans!

Let's move!

11.30 A.M. Eventually, the deadlock begins to break.

By the end of the day, the men are 1.6 kilometres (1 mile) inland. Of the 34,000 men who landed, over 2,500 are dead, wounded, or missing.

Some troops manage to force a path around the German strongholds, which becomes an escape route for the soldiers on the beach.

UTAH BEACH

6.30 A.M.

Taken by the US Army's 4th Division, Utah proves to be the easiest of all the Allied landings. The success is due in part to the 101st Airborne. After parachuting in during the night, it holds the land inland of the beaches and keeps the Germans from counterattacking the main invasion force.

At Utah, the Americans manage to get 28 of their 32 tanks ashore, by launching them much closer to the beach than those of the first wave at Omaha.

The soldiers land at Utah about 1.6 kilometres (1 mile) south of where they'd planned to, but this turns out to be lucky. The German position in the planned location is much more heavily fortified.

That's crazy! Swimming tanks? I must be seeing things!

Are we in the right place?

Beats me!

Lt. Richard "Dick" Winters of the 101st Airborne is ordered to attack four huge German guns on Utah Beach.

He takes 10 men to assault the position, which is heavily fortified and held by a 50-man German crew.

Winters and his men destroy all four guns.

They kill or capture more than half of the German soldiers.

Today, this attack is used by the United States Military Academy to teach cadets how to attack an entrenched position.

Leading the 4th Division on Utah is Brigadier General Theodore Roosevelt Jr, son of the president of the same name. He uses a cane because he has arthritis and a heart condition, and wears a knit cap because he hates helmets.

Roosevelt realizes they are in the wrong landing zone, but since his men are already moving inland, he decides to take advantage of the situation.

7.10 A.M.

A major threat to troops landing on Utah Beach and Omaha Beach is Pointe du Hoc, a rocky piece of land that juts out into the sea. It offers clear firing on the beaches below.

The Allies believe there are six German artillery guns held there. It is an obvious target, but the problem is that the guns sit atop a 30-metre- (100-foot-) high cliff...

...that is guarded by enemy forces.

The Americans send special troops, called Rangers, to attack the enemy.

But as the Rangers start climbing up the cliff, Germans drop grenades on them from above and cut their grapnel lines.

They use ladders and fire climbing ropes attached to hooks, called grapnels, to get to the top of the cliffs.

Keep your head down!

However, after 15 minutes of climbing, the Rangers reach the top. Once there, they have to fight off the German forces.

To their surprise, there are no guns at Pointe du Hoc, only telephone poles put out to fool the Allied air reconnaissance. The Germans had moved the guns inland.

So where are the big guns?

Don't worry. We'll find 'em.

One British general, Lord Lovat of Scotland, brings his bagpiper along. He and his men have to fight their way off the beach. Their mission is to meet up with the airborne forces already inland.

SCREEEEECH

1.10 P.M.

Lovat and his commandos reach the Caen Canal and Orne Bridge later that day. They provide the extra support needed to secure the bridges permanently.

I knew it wasn't an enemy once I heard the bagpipes!

The British land 29,000 men on Sword with just 630 casualties.

7:30 A.M.

The British landing at Gold Beach is almost an hour later than the American landings due to different tides. This is fortunate for the landing troops, as it gives the bombers and battleships longer to pound the German defences, most of which are severely damaged.

Most of the Allies' casualties and damage to equipment is caused by obstacles placed by the Germans. These include mines and obstructions to keep the tanks from moving forward.

Just crunch over the obstacles. They won't stop you from beaching. And don't worry about how you're going to get out. The main thing is to land.

7.45 A.M.

The Canadian troops attacking Juno Beach are supposed to land at 7.30 a.m., but the tide delays them. By the time the force approaches the beach, the tide has covered many of the German obstacles.

Some boats have their bottoms ripped off; others are blown up by unseen mines.

Due to the delay, there is a longer bombardment of the Germans to weaken their defence. However, in this case, the Germans do not suffer much damage and return to their posts once the shelling has stopped.

All the naval attack has done is let the Germans know we're coming!

Like the British troops, the Canadians landed with "funnies" to support their attack.

FUNNIES

"Funnies" were machines that had special features to assist the Allies. They were devised by British general Percy Hobart. The crab, or flail tank, had long chains that would flail to detonate mines in its path. The ark funny was a tank without a turret that had extendable ramps at each end. Other vehicles could drive up the ramps to scale obstacles. Other funnies included a flamethrower tank and the Assault Vehicle, Royal Engineers (AVRE), which could shoot an 18-kilogram (40-pound) bomb to break down concrete barriers

At Juno, 21,400 men are put ashore with 1,200 casualties – second only to Omaha. However, the Canadians make their way deeper into France than any other division.

SUMMARY

As D-Day ended, the soldiers on the beaches might not have known that it was the end of Nazi Germany's hold on Europe. But Field Marshal Rommel saw it. Surveying the entrenched Allies the day after the invasion, he told his aide that if he were commander of the Allied forces right now, he could finish off the war in 14 days.

The Allies soon began an endless delivery of reinforcements. There were more troops, more supplies, more tanks, more heavy guns, and more ammunition. The beaches were a traffic jam of vehicles and cargo unloading from the landing ships. The British constructed remarkable artificial harbours, called Mulberries, off Omaha Beach and Arromanches. That way even more ships could dock and unload. There was no stopping the Allies. But the Germans certainly tried.

Snipers and artillery fire rained on the crews unloading the ships. At first, there was still an enemy-held gap between Omaha Beach and Utah Beach, but by 12 June, all five beaches were joined in an uninterrupted Allied line covering 80 kilometres (50 miles) of Normandy coastline. The Allies had won the battle of the beaches, and they were also winning the battle of supplies.

Nonetheless, going into the French countryside from the beaches proved to be a big problem for the Allies. Normandy farmers had built an intricate patchwork of high hedgerows and narrow roads to separate their fields. These obstacles provided great cover for German machine guns, snipers, and tanks. The Allies had to fight their battles from hedgerow to hedgerow. Progress was slow, but an inventive American sergeant came up with an idea to outfit the Allied Sherman tanks with blades to let the tanks cut right through the hedgerows. By 24 July, US troops under General Omar Bradley had finally broken out of Normandy. Now the Allied forces could race across France. On 25 August, the Allies entered Paris. On 3 September, they entered the Belgian cities of Brussels and Antwerp.

As 1944 drew to a close, the Allies were ready to push into Germany. But the troops were exhausted and overstretched. And though weakened by long years of fighting, the Germans were still a challenging enemy. On 16 December, they launched a counterattack, later named the Battle of the Bulge because of the giant bulge it created in the Allied line. The US troops retreated in confusion, in the wintry fog and snow. But once the skies cleared a week later, the Allies' superior air force devastated the German tanks and troops with bomb attacks. Also, the Germans were running out of fuel for their tanks. The Battle of the Bulge was over by the end of January 1945. The Allies had won again, and they moved into Germany. Meanwhile, the Soviets were approaching from the East.

There was no escape for Germany. The country was in chaos, and Hitler directed what was left of his forces from a bunker in Berlin. On 30 April 1945, he committed suicide. On 7 May, Germany unconditionally surrendered. The war in Europe was finally over.

TIMELINE

6 June 1944

12.00 a.m.	Thousands of Allied paratroopers fly across the English Channel in planes, ready to begin the invasion of France
12.15 a.m.	First paratroopers begin to land in Normandy
12.30 a.m.	British troops from one of the first gliders to land capture two critical bridges over the Caen Canal and the Orne River
2.30 a.m.	Paratroopers from the 82nd Airborne Division begin to land. One company lands in the German-occupied town of Ste. Mère-Église.
3.00 a.m.	Allied bombers begin their aerial attack on the German beach defences
4.00 a.m	American paratroopers capture the town of Ste. Mère-Église
5.50 a.m.	Naval bombardment of Omaha and Utah beaches begins
6.00 a.m.	Naval bombardment of Sword, Juno, and Gold beaches begins
6.30 a.m.	American troops land on Omaha Beach and Utah Beach
7.10 a.m.	US rangers begin assault on Pointe du Hoc
7.25 a.m.	British troops land on Sword Beach
7.30 a.m.	British troops land on Gold Beach
7.45 a.m.	Canadian troops land on Juno Beach
8.16 a.m.	Sword Beach: British troops begin to move clear of the beach and advance inland
8.30 a.m.	Gold Beach: German defences are giving way all along the beach

The times given in this book are approximate and may vary between sources.

9.15 a.m.	Omaha Beach: American losses are so heavy that General Omar Bradley considers abandoning the mission
9.30 a.m.	Juno Beach: First wave of Canadian forces are clear of the beach and advancing inland
11.30 a.m.	Omaha Beach: American forces clear an exit to escape from the beach
12.00 p.m.	Utah Beach: 101st Airborne Division, which includes Lieutenant Richard "Dick" Winters and his men, secures four vital positions off Utah Beach
1.00 p.m.	Utah Beach: US Army's 4th Division advances inland and meets up with 101st Airborne Division
1.10 p.m.	Sword Beach: British ground forces, led by Lord Lovat, meet up with airborne troops inland
8.00 p.m.	Gold Beach: British advance stops for the night. They have reached 9.7 kilometres (6 miles) inland, and joined up with the Canadian forces from Juno Beach.
8.30 p.m.	Juno Beach: Canadian advance stops for the night. They have reached 11.3 kilometres (7 miles) inland – the furthest of all the forces.
9.00 p.m.	Large Allied air fleet arrives on the Normandy coast carrying reinforcements
11.00 p.m.	Sword Beach: British advance on Caen stops for the night. They are 9.7 kilometres (6 miles) inland.
7 June, 12.00 a.m.	All beachheads have been secured. Many objectives remain unachieved, but the Allies have a foothold in Nazi Europe. Operation Overlord has been a resounding success.
7 May	Germany surrenders to the Allies
2 September	Japan formally surrenders, ending the war

CAST OF CHARACTERS

Dwight D. Eisenhower (1890–1969)
Before World War II, Eisenhower was a US Army colonel who was getting ready to retire. But by 1943, Eisenhower (now a general) was serving as supreme commander of the Allied forces in Europe and was responsible for the massive Normandy D-Day invasion in 1944. After the war, "Ike" (as he was called) became so popular that he was elected president of the United States twice – in 1952 and again in 1956.

Theodore Roosevelt Jr (1887–1944)
The son of President Theodore Roosevelt, Brigadier General Theodore Roosevelt Jr, was, at 56, the oldest man to land on D-Day. He was also the only general to lead his troops onto a Normandy beach. Roosevelt had arthritis and walked with a cane. He also suffered from heart trouble, and died of a heart attack in France just a few weeks after the invasion. He was posthumously awarded the Medal of Honor, the United States' highest military honour, for his actions on Utah Beach.

Omar Bradley (1893–1981)
General Bradley had already led troops to victory in North Africa and Sicily when Eisenhower picked him to command the 1st US Army during D-Day. Bradley oversaw the landings at Omaha Beach and Utah Beach. As more soldiers continued to arrive in Normandy after the invasion, Bradley was given a new command, the 12th Army Group, which grew to 1.3 million men. It became the largest group of American soldiers to ever serve under one field commander. Bradley was also the last promoted US Army five-star general.

Bernard Law Montgomery (1887–1976)

Montgomery led the British Eighth Army in North Africa, where he was the first Allied general to inflict a serious defeat upon the Axis forces at El Alamein. After his victories there, "Monty" (as he was known) worked closely with Eisenhower to plan the D-Day invasion of Normandy. Montgomery commanded all ground forces in the initial stages of the invasion. In 1944 he was made a field marshal, the highest rank in the British Army. After the war, he was made 1st Viscount Montgomery of Alamein.

Erwin Rommel (1891–1944)

Field Marshal Rommel was known as the Desert Fox due to his skilled leadership of the Afrika Korps, the German forces in the North African campaign of World War II. In 1944 he was charged to defend the French coast from Allied invasion. He ordered millions of mines and thousands of traps and obstacles set up on the coast and the countryside to hinder an Allied attack. He was unable to repel the D-Day invasion. Later in the war, Rommel was implicated in a plot to kill Hitler. Rommel had the choice to stand trial or take poison. He agreed to commit suicide to keep his family safe.

Adolf Hitler (1889–1945)

Hitler was the founder and leader of the Nazi Party. He was the military and political leader of Germany from 1933 to 1945. He annexed Austria and took over part of Czechoslovakia. Then he invaded Poland in 1939 which launched World War II. Soon Hitler had much of Europe in his grasp. During this time, Hitler was responsible for some of the most terrible crimes in history. He began rounding up and killing millions of Jews and other people whom the Nazis considered inferior. But the Allies fought back against the Germans. They successfully invaded Normandy, and the Russians fought back on the Eastern Front. Squeezed between his enemies and knowing defeat was inevitable, Hitler committed suicide in his Berlin bunker in April 1945.

GLOSSARY

aerial of or happening in the air

alliance group of countries who join together to achieve a common goal

annex make part of an existing nation or city

artillery heavy guns and cannon

barrage heavy concentration of fire

beachhead initial position on a beach that invading troops try to secure when landing on an enemy shore

bombardment attack using artillery or bombers

bomber aeroplane for dropping bombs

bunker fortified underground shelter used by soldiers in wartime

casualty person in the armed forces who is killed or injured in war

civilian person not in active duty in a military force

commando member of a military unit trained for surprise raids

destroyer small, speedy warship

dictator ruler who has total power over a country

diversion something intended to distract attention from something more important

division group of army brigades or regiments

fortify strengthen a position to make it defensible against a military attack

Führer leader, especially a tyrant

glider aircraft resembling an aeroplane but having no engine

grapnel small anchor with usually four claws used especially in dragging or grappling operations

infantry soldiers on foot

mine hidden explosive device used to destroy enemy personnel, vehicles, or ships

minesweeper warship designed for removing or neutralizing underwater mines

naval of or relating to a navy

oberleutnant junior officer rank in the German military

paratrooper soldier trained to jump out of an aeroplane using a parachute

posthumous occurring after one's death

reconnaissance examination of an area, to gain useful military information

regiment military unit consisting usually of a number of battalions

repulse drive back an attacking enemy by force

sabotage destroy or hamper actions by enemy agents or sympathizers in time of war

FIND OUT MORE

Books

D-Day (My Story), Bryan Perrett (Scholastic, 2009)

Life in World War II (Unlocking History), Brian Williams (Raintree, 2010)

Normandy: A Graphic History of D-Day, Wayne Vansant (Zenith Press, 2012)

World War II (Living Through...), Andrew Langley (Raintree, 2012)

World War II: The Definitive Visual Guide, Richard Holmes (Dorling Kindersley, 2009)

DVDs

The Longest Day (20th Century Fox, 1962)

This film, based on the book by Cornelius Ryan, recreates the D-Day landings from the perspective of the Allies and the Germans, and focuses on both the large and small events of that historic day.

Websites

www.bbc.co.uk/history/worldwars/wwtwo

Visit the BBC's site on World War II, which includes a special section on D-Day and Operation Overlord. There you can listen to the voices of people who experienced D-Day first-hand, see an interactive animation of the landings, and much more.

www.britannica.com/dday

For a good introduction to D-Day, check out Encyclopedia Britannica's guide to Normandy 1944, where you'll find a photo gallery, see interactive charts and maps, and watch combat videos, too.

www.ddaymuseum.co.uk/d-day/the-museum
Check out the Portsmouth D-Day Museum's website. It's a fantastic resource that covers the preparation for the big day, the channel crossing, as well as all the beach landings, and answers all your D-Day questions as well.

www.pbs.org/wgbh/amex/dday/index.html
If you want to see an American take on D-Day, look at this PBS site. Read letters that soldiers sent home, see what paratroopers carried in their packs, and even read newspaper reports from the time.

Places to visit

D-Day Museum and Overlord Embroidery
Clarence Esplanade
Southsea
PO5 3NT
www.ddaymuseum.co.uk/d-day/the-museum
Established in 1984 to tell the story of Operation Overlord, the D-Day Museum in Portsmouth is the UK's only museum dedicated solely to the D-Day landings. The Museum's centerpiece is the 83-metre long Overlord Embroidery, inspired by the Bayeux Tapestry. Thirty-four embroidered panels depict the Allies' efforts to overcome Nazi Germany.

Battle Sites of Normandy, France
Many people visit the D-Day beaches, where wreckage from the battles can still be seen. In Normandy, you can visit the town of Ste. Mère-Église and its Airborne Museum, as well as pay respect to fallen soldiers at the cemetery overlooking Omaha Beach. It is possible to arrange for a professionally guided tour, but you can always get your own copy of a battlefield guide if you prefer.

INDEX